MW01635471

FACTS AT YOUR FINGERTIPS

THE SEA

ORIOLE PARK
SCHOOL LIBRARY
RED DEER, A[illegible]TA

DAVID MARSHALL

SIMON & SCHUSTER
YOUNG BOOKS

Commissioning editor: Daphne Butler
Design and artwork: SPL Design
Photographs: ZEFA, except for
NHPA (10b, 12b, 15t, 17br)
Robert Harding (5m, 9t, 13, 17tr, 17l, 21t, 25t)
Typesetting and layout: Quark Xpress

First published in Great Britain in 1992
by Simon & Schuster Young Books

Simon & Schuster Young Books
Campus 400, Maylands Avenue
Hemel Hempstead, Herts HP2 7EZ

© 1992 Simon & Schuster Young Books

All rights reserved

Printed and bound in Belgium
by Proost International Book Production

A catalogue record for this book
is available from the British Library
ISBN 0 7500 1085 1

CONTENTS

ORIOLE PARK
SCHOOL LIBRARY
RED DEER, ALBERTA

4

WHAT ARE

THE SEAS?

About three-quarters of the Earth's surface is covered by oceans and seas. Long ago, as the Earth cooled, steam rose from the surface and turned to clouds. These rained torrents of water down on to the Earth forming the seas and oceans. ►

◄ The oceans are deep and mysterious. Tales of monsters and lost cities abound. People first reached the very bottom of the oceans about thirty years ago. For most of us, it is a strange, unknown world.

The water in the seas is in constant motion. It evaporates to form clouds. These drop rain on the land which returns in rivers to the sea—the same sea where life began and dinosaurs drowned, where Columbus sailed and many love to swim. ►

SEAS AND OCEANS

The largest ocean is the Pacific which covers about a third of the Earth's surface. The other great oceans are the Atlantic, Indian, Southern and Arctic oceans. Some parts of oceans have special names, like the Sargasso Sea in the Atlantic Ocean.

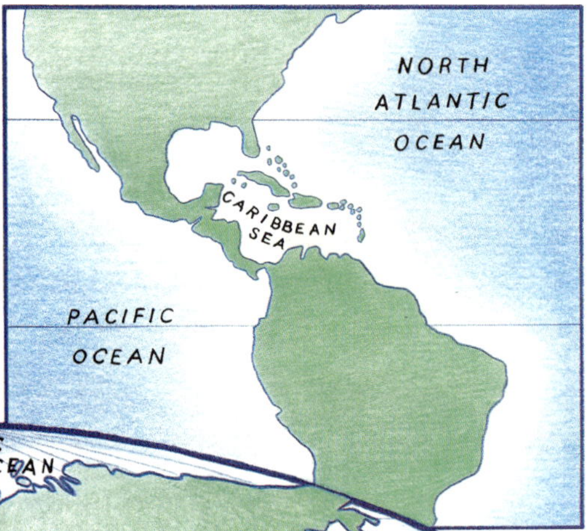

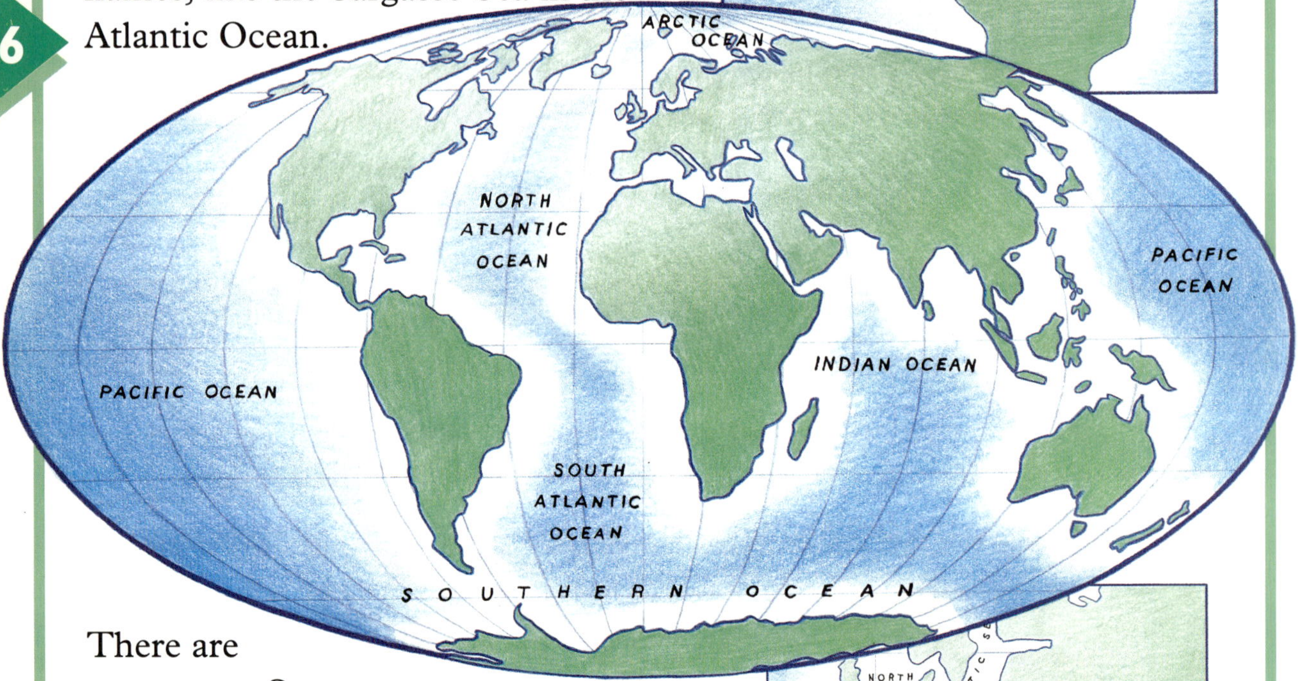

There are many seas. Some seas are shallow—for example the North Sea and the Baltic Sea. Others are surrounded by land, like the Black, Red, and Caspian Seas, and the best known of all, the Mediterranean—which the Romans called "in the middle of lands".

THE OCEAN FLOOR

The Ocean floor is very uneven, and not at all like the level, sandy beach where you paddle. Under the sea, towering cliffs give way to very deep trenches. There are mountain ranges with volcanoes and canyons, and in other places flat plains.

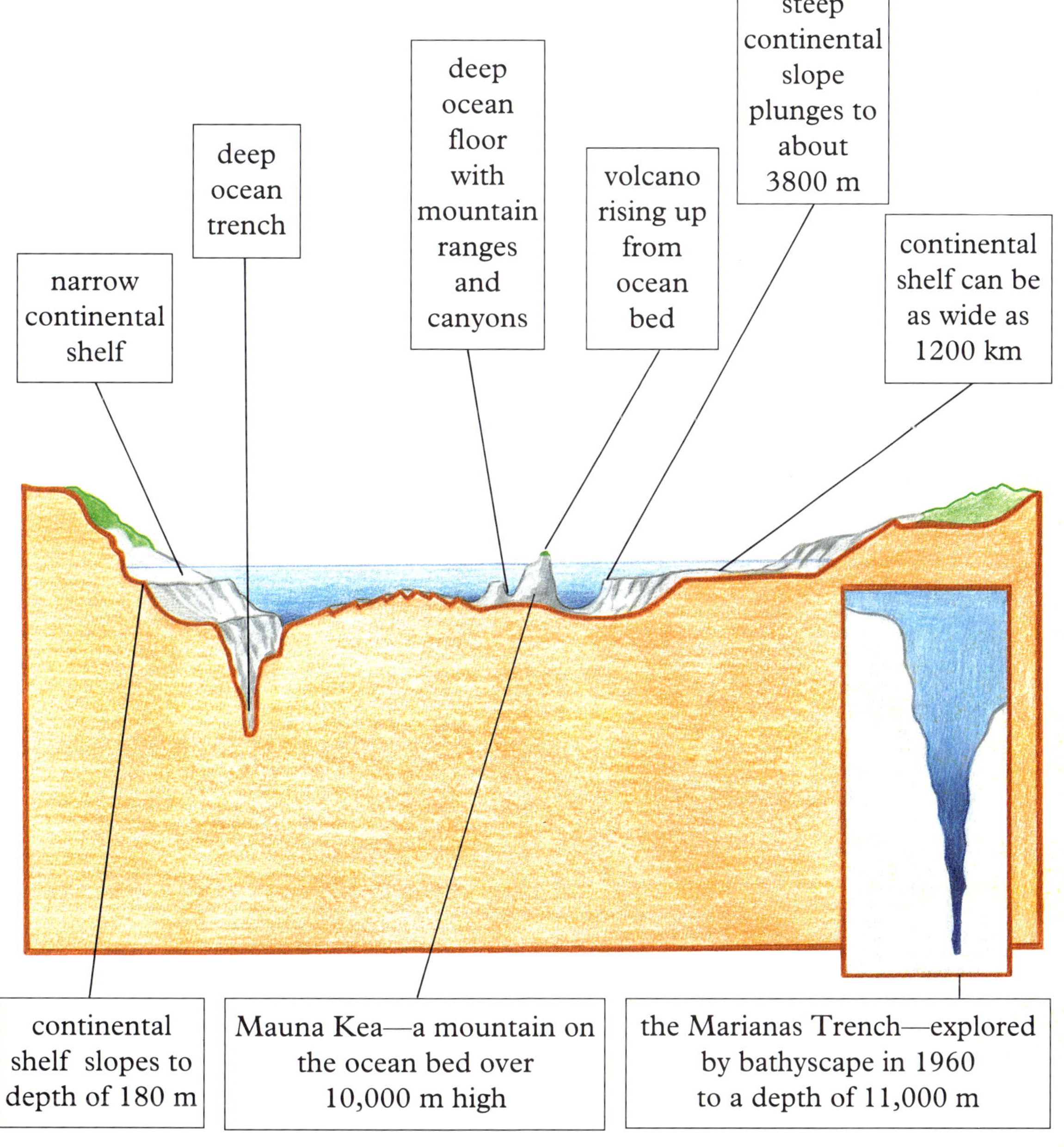

WAVES

Waves are caused by wind blowing across the surface of the sea. The water moves up and down as the wave passes through. Crests tumble over slower moving water below, especially over shallow water dragging on the shore.

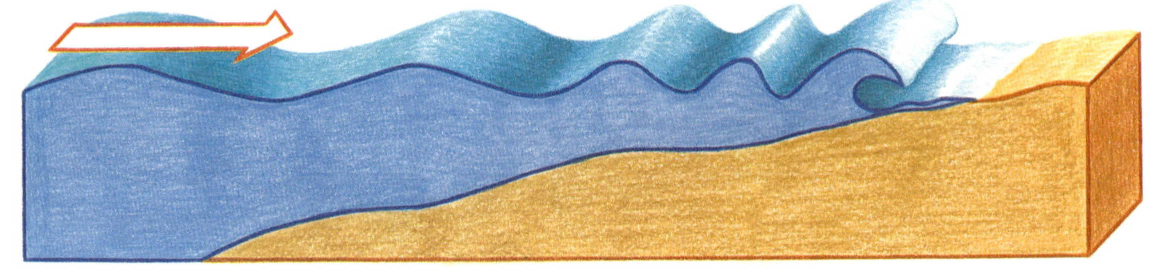

CURRENTS

Powerful currents flow across the oceans mixing icy polar waters with the warm surface waters near the equator. They are caused partly by the prevailing winds and partly by the spin of the Earth. The currents flow clockwise in the northern half of the world and anti-clockwise in the southern half. Cold water is heavier than warm, and sinks, making deep ocean currents freezing cold.

▲Boats stranded by the falling tide. There is often a big difference between high and low tide in narrow bays or channels.

TIDES

Tides rise and fall twice in every twenty-five hours, but occur about an hour later each time. They are caused by the pull of the sun and the moon on the ocean waters. In an enclosed sea like the Mediterrranean the difference between high and low tide is only about 30 centimetres, but in the open ocean it can be up to a metre.

Spring tides occur near the time of full moon and new moon, when the sun and moon are lined up so they pull on the water together. Spring tides have the biggest rise and fall. ►

Neap tides occur when the moon is in its first and last quarters when the sun and moon are pulling at right angles to each other. Neap tides have a much smaller range than spring tides. ►

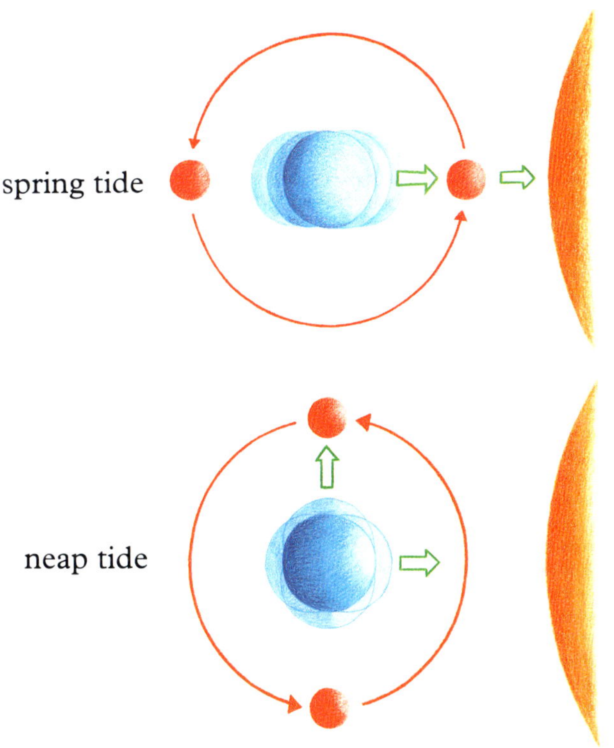

EROSION

Waves pick up stones and sand and pound them against the cliffs slowly wearing the rocks away. The sea carves out bays in softer rocks, leaving harder rocks sticking out as headlands or stacks.

Constant erosion slowly grinds rocky cliffs to sand. The sand is light and easily carried along by the water. It may be deposited as sand banks or blown up on the shore as dunes.

▲ Jagged rocks—the Irish coastline pounded by the Atlantic Ocean.

◄ Marram grass takes root on the dunes—sand washed up on the Welsh coast.

VOLCANOES AND REEFS

Volcanoes often erupt along underwater mountain ridges, forming new islands when they are high enough to show above the surface. In November 1963, a new island which is now called Surtsey, suddenly appeared off Iceland. Within a few days, Surtsey was 61 metres high and 610 metres long. Within two years the first green plants started to grow, and fivc years later, there were more than 20 species of birds and insects living there.

Volcanic eruption under water ▼

Coral rccfs form around volcanic islands in warm sunlit waters. Over a long period of time the reef circles the island. ▼

SALTINESS

If two cupfuls of salt are dissolved in a bucket of water, it is as salty as seawater

Seawater is always salty because rainwater dissolves the salts in rocks and carries them down to the sea.

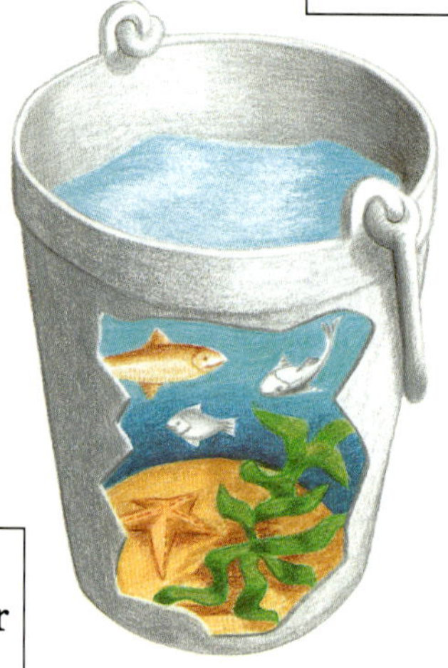

The Dead Sea is so salty that no animals or plants can live there.

Seawater freezes at a lower temperature than fresh water because it contains salts.

In hot countries, salt is made by evaporating shallow pools of seawater in the heat of the sun.

Warm seas are saltier than cold ones.

FROZEN SEA

The frozen waters of the Arctic and Antarctic are even colder than a frozen lake. The Arctic is frozen water surrounded by land and the Antarctic is frozen land surrounded by the icy Southern Ocean. The Antarctic ice covers nearly a tenth of the Earth's surface.

Sometimes huge pieces of ice break away from the ice caps and form icebergs. Icebergs are dangerous to shipping because only an eighth of their bulk shows above the water, often shrouded by mist.

EXPLORING THE SEA

The first scientific exploration of the oceans was in 1872 when *HMS Challenger* spent three years travelling around the world. The scientists on board discovered over 4,000 new species of plants and animals. The oceans are explored nowadays by divers, small submarines and taking satellite pictures.

Most scuba divers can only safely explore the top 50 metres of the ocean. They wear light protective clothing, carry their own air supply and can swim around with ease. ➤

LIVING IN

THE SEA

There are about 22,000 species of fish of which about 60 per cent live in the seas and oceans. This is more than all the species of mammals, birds, reptiles and amphibians combined. ►

◄ Whales have lived in the seas for about 65 million years. They are intelligent, warm-blooded and breathe air. Dolphins belong to a group of whales with teeth. They can have as many as 200 cone-shaped teeth.

Small plants known as algae have grown in the sea for 3.5 thousand million years. They give off oxygen and without algae animals would not have developed. Algae are important in helping to keep the level of oxygen in the air constant. ►

FOOD CHAIN

All life in the sea depends on tiny plants called phytoplankton which float near the surface close to the light where they can grow. Tiny animals called zooplankton feed on these plants. Krill are tiny plankton animals on which larger fish feed. Sea-birds and seals feed on large fish. Adelie penguins feed almost entirely on krill and it is also the main food for many sorts of whales and seals.

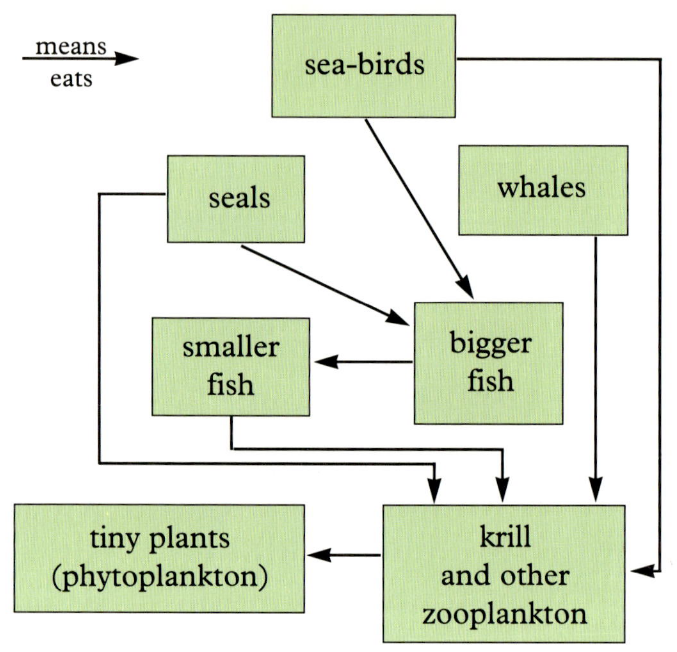

SEAWEEDS

Seaweed only grows in shallow water because like most plants it needs sunlight to help make its food. Some seaweeds are tiny tufts just a few millimetres in length, others, like the giant kelps off California can grow over 60 metres long.

Seaweed is green, red, brown or yellow. It has a foot called a holdfast which anchors it to the rocks and stops it being washed out to sea.

In some parts of the world seaweed is harvested as a vegetable. It is also used in making ice cream, toothpaste, paints, glue and medicines!

CORAL REEFS

▲ Soft coral polyps.

▲ Staghorn coral.

Gorgonia coral with polyps expanded. ▼

Gorgonia coral. ▼

All corals are formed from millions of skeletons of small sea animals called polyps. The hard covering of chalky material round each tiny polyp forms the reef. Although a coral reef may be huge, only the top surface is living coral. The coral underneath is dead.

Coral reefs need shallow water in warm seas with plenty of sunlight. They have been growing for 45 million years. A great variety of sea life lives in and around coral reefs.

Angel fish on coral reef. ▼

FISH

There are many thousand different kinds of fish. Over 22,000 species have been discovered but there are probably many more. Here are some that live in the sea.

sea bass
720 mm long

white basking shark 10 metres long

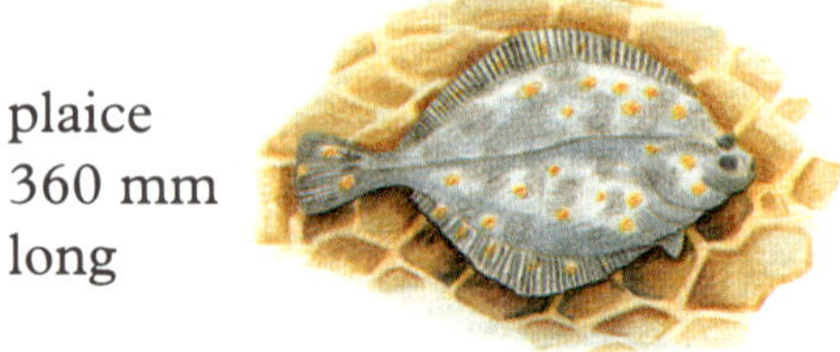

cod
720 mm long

plaice
360 mm long

dory
360 mm long

roker
720 mm long

conger eel
1.5 metres long

BIRDS AND SEA MAMMALS

◄ The puffin is only one of about 300 different species of sea-birds. Sea-birds fly easily over the waves on long tapered wings, diving into the sea to catch fish. They drink seawater and have special glands which draw the salt from their blood. Most spend their lives close to land coming together to nest in colonies on cliffs and in sand dunes. Others, like the albatross, spend lonely lives wandering the oceans.

▲ Killer whales are one of a group of sea mammals which includes baleen whales, seals, dolphins, porpoises, sea-lions, walruses and dugongs.

◄ Seals, like whales, have a thick layer of blubber to keep them warm in icy waters.

DORIS

HOW WE USE

THE SEA

It was more than 10,000 years ago that the first dug-out canoe was made from a tree trunk. Now we use ships and boats of all shapes and sizes to move people and goods around the world. ➤

◄ We have learnt how to survive under the sea. Exploring this underwater world gives some people great pleasure, and for others it is a chance to take riches from the oceans.

ORIOLE PARK
SCHOOL LIBRARY
RED DEER, ALBERTA

The treasures are immense. There are valuable minerals on the sea bed and in the rocks, fish in abundance and a wide variety of other beautiful and amazing things—it is one of the Earth's greatest natural resources. ➤

FUN AT SEA

The sea is a great source of pleasure. It is ever-changing—sometimes wild and exhilarating, at other times still and quiet.

It's good fun to play in the waves, to sail a boat in a strong breeze, race along on a sail board, or to ride the surf. It is lovely to stroll along the water's edge or paddle in the cool water on a hot day; to breathe in the fresh wind and smell the tang of the salt in the air; to search for shells at high water mark, or poke around in rock pools.

Whatever you like doing, the sea has something to offer.

Dinghies sailing in a race. The racers have hoisted large colourful sails called spinnakers to gain as much speed as possible from the light wind blowing the boats along from behind. ➤

FISHING

People used to think that there would always be plenty of fish in the seas for us to harvest, but this is not so. Fish that used to be commonplace are now scarce. Many parts of the seas have been so over-fished that there are very few fish living there.

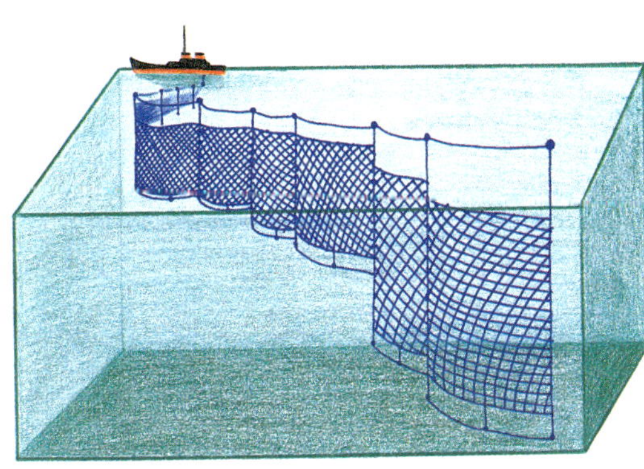

PURSE SEINE ►
Fish are circled by a curtain of net, the bottom is closed and the net hauled on to the boat.

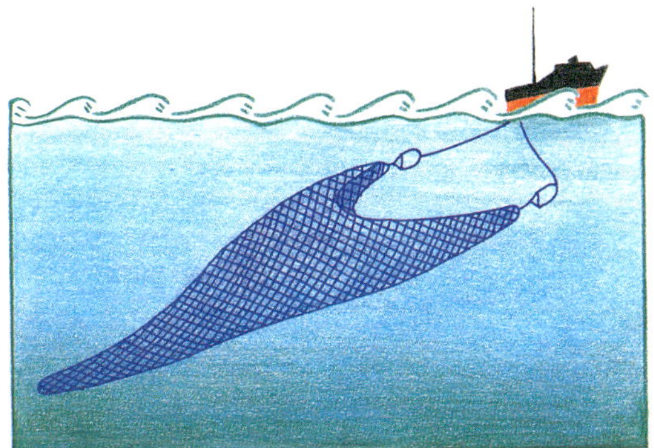

▲ Every year more than 60 million tonnes of fish are caught for us to eat.

◄ DRIFTING
Fine-mesh drift nets hang down from floats on the surface and are often many metres long. Any creature that swims into them is tangled up and caught. Drift nets catch millions of fish but also seals, whales and dolphins which die unnecessarily.

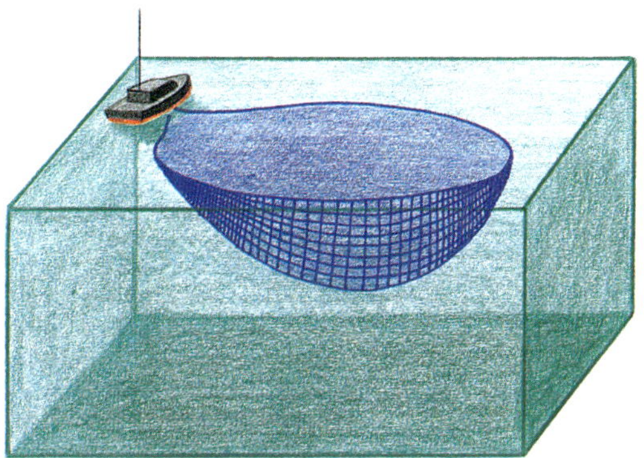

◄ TRAWLING
Many fish are caught in large nets, called trawls which drag across the ocean floor.

TRANSPORT

When Francis Drake set off around the world in 1577, his ship the *Golden Hind* was just 36 metres long, made of wood and powered by sails. The voyage lasted three years. Ships have changed greatly in the 400 years since. They are now made out of steel, powered by turbines and designed for the particular load they are to carry, like refrigerated container ships.

The largest ship built in modern times is an oil tanker called the *Seawise Giant.* It is 458 metres long and weighs over 570 thousand tonnes.

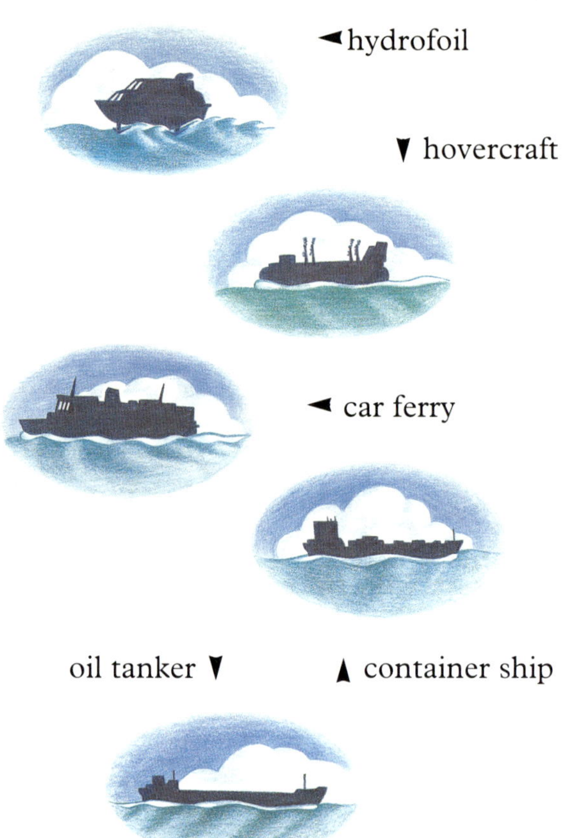

◄ hydrofoil

▼ hovercraft

◄ car ferry

oil tanker ▼

▲ container ship

Cargo ship with computer-controlled sails which help to save fuel. ▼

SAFETY AND THE SEA

The sea is beautiful but very dangerous. Ever since the *Titanic* sank in 1915 drowning 1500 people, large ships have carried life-jacket and lifebelts for every passenger as well as lifeboats with radio, drinking water and medical supplies. Modern rescue services use radar and planes to find survivors and helicopters which can winch people straight out of the sea.

DRINKING WATER FROM THE SEA

It is very expensive to make fresh water out of seawater, but worth it for very hot countries with only a little rainfall. One way is to boil the seawater and turn it to steam. The salt does not boil, so if you can 'catch' the steam as it cools down, it condenses back into pure water. This process is known as distillation and is carried out in factories known as desalination plants. The salt that is left behind is usually sold. Over 6 million tonnes of salt are taken from the sea each year.

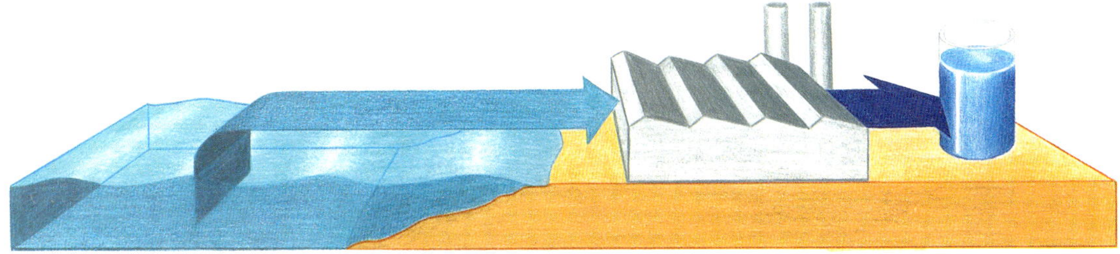

Water is pumped out of the sea.

It is passed into a desalination plant where the salt is removed.

Fresh water is stored in tanks.

FISH FARMING

Shellfish, particularly oysters, have been farmed for a long time, but other sea fish have been farmed only for about the last 40 years. Fish farming is expensive and is only worthwhile for fish such as trout, salmon and turbot which sell at a high price in the markets.

Salmon and trout can be kept in seawater once they reach a length of 15 centimetres—although their early life has to be spent in fresh water. The young fish are fed automatically in large tanks and then moved through a series of ponds. Plaice and sole are also farmed in tanks in the open sea. This speeds up their growth, and they reach full size in half the usual time.

◄ Salmon farming in Norway. In a sheltered fjord, the young fish are moved from pond to pond until they have grown big enough to send to market.

TREASURE FROM THE SEA

Clams and oysters sometimes get irritating pieces inside their shells which they cover with layers of a hard white chemical, calcium carbonate, forming pearls. The biggest pearl ever found came from a giant clam in the Philippines and is called the Pearl of Lao-Tze. It has the shape of a human brain and weighs over 6 kilogrammes.

Pearls are sorted and graded before being used for jewellery. ►

▲ The *Vergulde Draeck* from Holland went down in 1656 with 8 chests of silver.

Many ships have been wrecked over the years, some carrying valuable cargo. In 1942, *HMS Edinburgh*, sank with a staggering £45 millions worth of gold bars aboard. People sometimes try to find these treasures and raise them from the seabed.

◄ In 1545, Henry VIII's flagship the *Mary Rose* sank off Portsmouth. In 1985, it was brought back to the surface, with many of its artefacts intact.

MINING UNDER THE SEA

◄ Offshore oil rigs are heavy awkward structures. They are floated out to the drilling position and then anchored to the sea bed. Some rigs stand on huge legs, others are tethered by hundreds of thick wires.

Crude oil is pumped into tankers and taken ashore. Gas lying on top of the oil is pumped straight to reservoir tanks on shore. ►

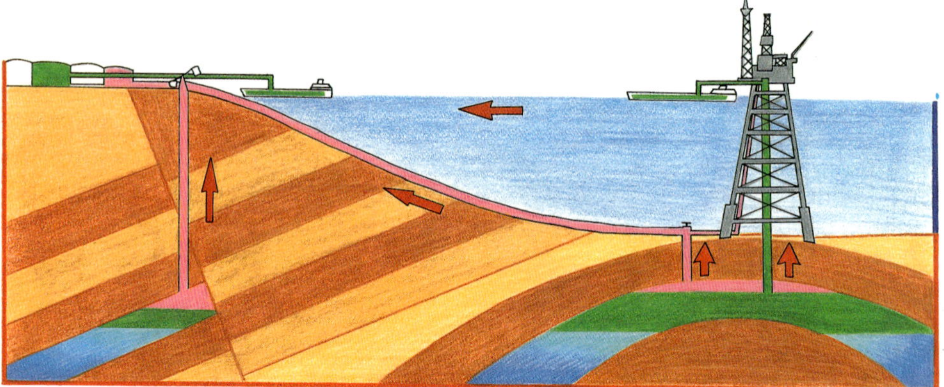

Over a fifth of the world's oil and gas comes from the rocks under the sea bed. Special off-shore platforms are used. A single oil rig in the North Sea produces enough oil in one day to make petrol to fill 70,000 cars. Scientists and engineers are also investigating ways of raising the many thousands of small black pebbles that lie on the Pacific Ocean floor. These pebbles contain many valuable minerals, like copper, nickel and cobalt, but they are very deep and expensive to retrieve.

POLLUTION AT SEA

In 1989, a huge oil tanker, called the *Exxon Valdez*, ran aground in the Alaskan Sea. Over 45 million litres of oil spilled out, and hundreds of thousands of fish, seals and sea birds died as a result. It was the worst oil spill ever, until the wanton pumping of oil into the sea off Kuwait during the Gulf War in 1991.

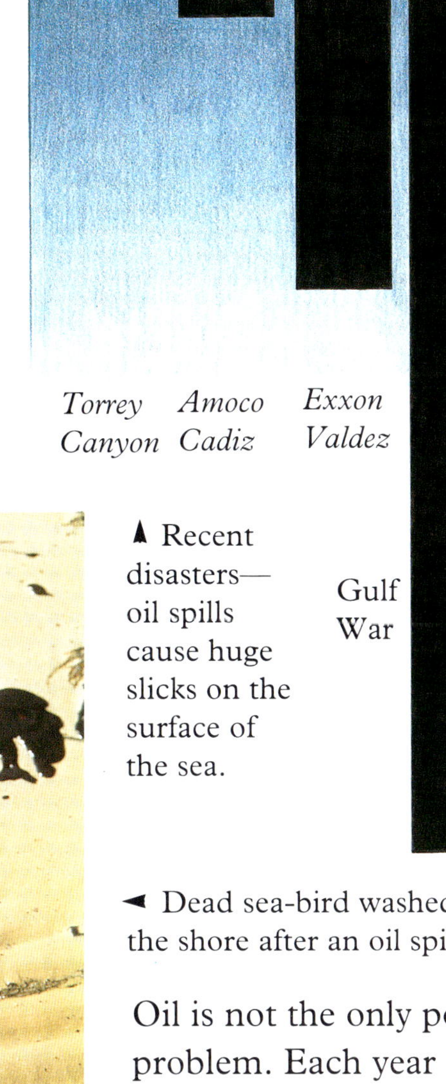

▲ Recent disasters—oil spills cause huge slicks on the surface of the sea.

◄ Dead sea-bird washed up on the shore after an oil spillage.

Oil is not the only pollution problem. Each year millions of kilogrammes of rubbish are dumped in the sea, much of it plastic—also raw sewage, and poisonous industrial and radioactive wastes.

FACTS ABOUT THE SEA

The largest iceberg ever recorded was 31,000 square kilometres—an area larger than Belgium.

The Bay of Fundy on the Atlantic coast of Canada has the greatest tides—a rise and fall of just over 15 metres.

The saltiest sea is the Dead Sea—10 times saltier than the oceans.

There are about 9 million tonnes of gold in the world's oceans.

The pygmy goby is the smallest sea fish—no longer than 9 mm.

The largest coral reef is the Great Barrier Reef off north-eastern Australia. It is about 2000 km long.

The highest storm wave ever recorded was in the Pacific Ocean. It was over 34 metres high.

The whale shark is the largest fish—15 metres long and weighing up to 15 tonnes.

The Pacific is the largest ocean—over 165 million square kilometres. The Arctic is the smallest just over 12 million square kilometres.

The coelacanth fish was rediscovered off East Africa in 1938. It was believed to have been extinct for 70 million years.

INDEX

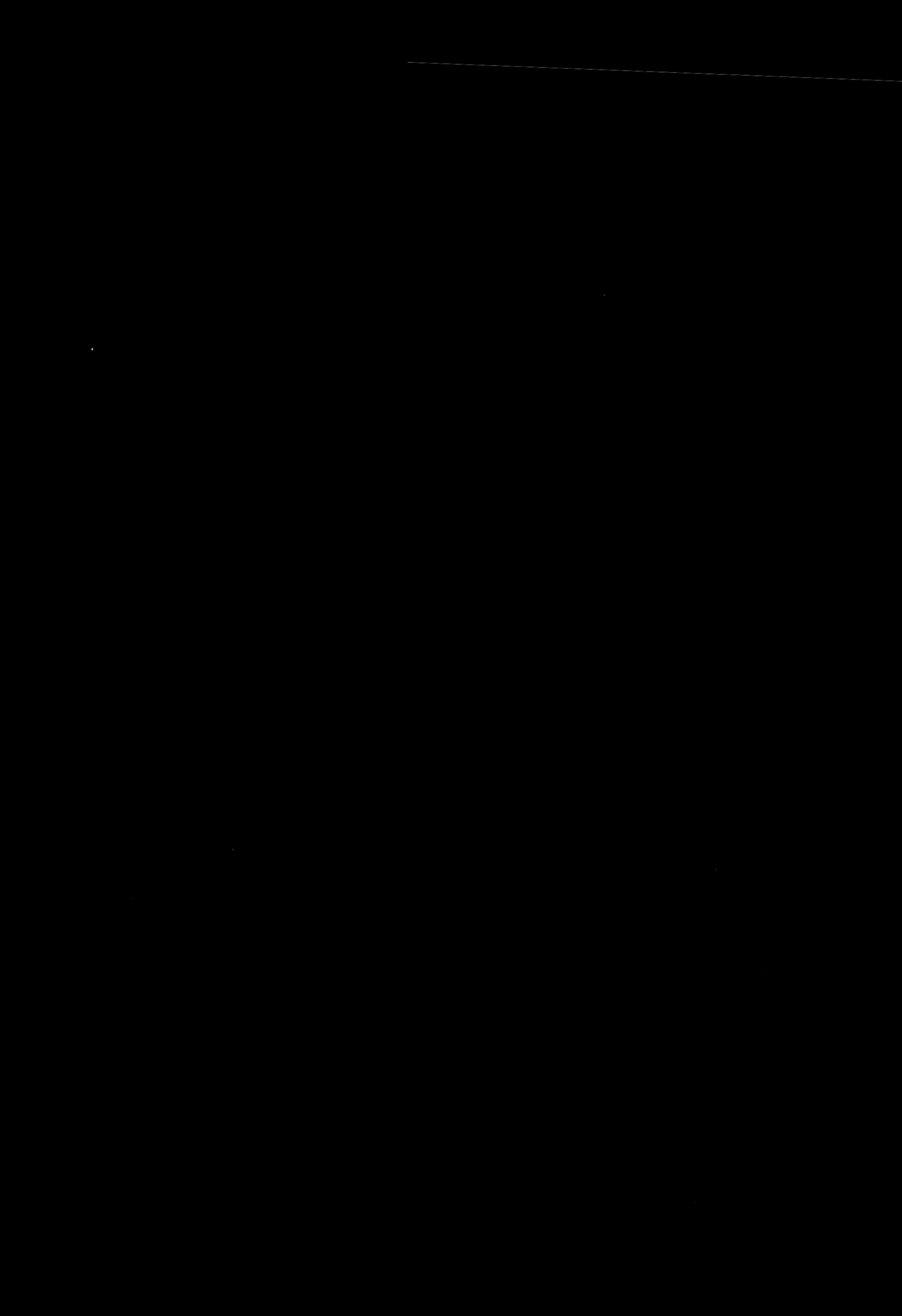